Practical
One Pot

p^3

This is a P³ Book
This edition published in 2004

P³
Queen Street House
4 Queen Street
Bath BA1 1HE, UK

ISBN: 1-40542-309-9

Manufactured in China

NOTE

Cup measurements in this book are for American cups.
This book also uses imperial and metric measurements. Follow the same units
of measurement throughout; do not mix imperial and metric.
All spoon measurements are level: teaspoons are assumed to be 5 ml, and
tablespoons are assumed to be 15 ml. Unless otherwise stated,
milk is assumed to be whole milk, eggs and individual vegetables such as potatoes
are medium, and pepper is freshly ground black pepper.

The nutritional information provided for each recipe is per serving or per person.
Optional ingredients, variations, or serving suggestions have
not been included in the calculations. The times given for each recipe are an approximate
guide only because the preparation times may differ according to the techniques used by
different people and the cooking times may vary as a result of the type of oven used.

Recipes using raw or very lightly cooked eggs should be
avoided by infants, the elderly, pregnant women, convalescents,
and anyone suffering from an illness.

Contents

Introduction

Casseroles, stews, and other one-pot meals are traditionally served in the winter, but there is no reason why you cannot enjoy these dishes all year round. One-pot cooking is not only suitable for meat dishes—fish, vegetables, and beans also benefit from this way of cooking. As well as the intense flavor that can be achieved, one-pot cooking is also an ideal way to cook cheaper cuts of meat, which can be very helpful to the family budget.

One-pot cooking

This cooking method involves simply placing all the ingredients in one pot and then simmering on the stove or in the oven. Pot roasting is also a form of one-pot cooking. When spices are involved, cook them gently prior to the liquid being added in order to ensure that they do not taste raw and spoil the finished taste.

When using a pot on the stove, choose a pot with a heavy bottom and close-fitting lid. The pot should be large enough so that it only needs to be filled to about three-fourths full, otherwise it may boil over. Use the simmering facility on the stove—if preferred, invest in a heat diffuser, which is available in two sizes, suitable for use on either gas or electric stoves.

If using a pot in the oven, make sure that, in addition to a heavy bottom and close-fitting lid, the pot has handles on both sides for easy removal. The handles should be well secured and ovenproof.

Casseroles

When you are casseroling you are employing a variety of cooking methods: stewing, steaming, and roasting. Choose cheaper cuts of meat for casseroles—it would be an extravagant waste of ingredients and money to use something expensive like fillet steak in a casserole. Meat and poultry are normally placed on a bed of vegetables and cooked with sufficient liquid to provide the steam to keep the food moist.

The ideal oven temperature is 325°F/160°C. The liquid within the pot needs to be kept simmering (just below boiling point). If the liquid is left to boil for any length of time, the finished dish could end up tough.

Stews

Stews are produced by long, slow cooking, with the ingredients immersed in a liquid that is kept below boiling point, at a temperature of 205°F/96°C. This method is normally used for the cheaper cuts of meat that require long, slow cooking in order to break down the connective tissue. With stews, the food is cut into bite-size pieces, whereas with casseroles, larger pieces are often used. The food to be stewed is normally seared either in oil or butter in order to preserve all the flavor and to ensure a good color.

Most international cuisines often have their own specialty cooking pots, which are designed specifically for local dishes. Tagine, for example, is a Moroccan specialty, where all the food is cooked in a tagine dish (see page 14).

Types of food used

Poultry and meat are the foods most commonly associated with stews and casseroles. When buying any of these, look for the following cuts.

Chicken: look out for boiling fowls—these often need ordering from farms or local butchers. These fowls have a slightly gamey flavor. When using oven-ready chickens, use the portions that are still on the bone.

Turkey: the dark meat is better for long, slow cooking—look out for packs of diced thigh meat, which is excellent in casseroles.

Duck and goose: these are very fatty and are not ideal in casseroles—if you do use them, let them cool after cooking, then skim off the fat before serving.

Game: this is ideal for stewing or cooking in a casserole and is well worth trying when in season. Pheasant can be quite tough if roasted and therefore often benefits from long, slow cooking, as do other game animals and birds such as hare, venison, and pigeon.

Beef: brisket, which is normally sold off the bone and rolled, is an ideal cut to use in a pot roast. It is reasonably fatty but with an intense meaty flavor. If salted, soak thoroughly first.

Silverside is a boneless joint, again often sold salted. It is the joint most commonly used in the traditional recipe of boiled beef and dumplings.

Flank is often sold as stewing steak, cut into small, bite-size pieces.

Leg and shin are used in stews and casseroles, and need the long, slow cooking to break down the connective tissue. These are usually among the cheapest cuts but have an excellent flavor.

Neck and clod are normally sold diced or ground—they are fairly lean but less gelatinous than shin.

Chuck of blade comes from the shoulder. It is a fairly lean cut of reasonable good quality and is most suitable for braising or casseroles.

Lamb: this is a very fatty meat. When using it in a casserole or stew, it is a good idea to let the finished dish cool so that the fat can easily be skimmed off.

Chump end chops are at the end of the chump and are unevenly shaped chops—often used for casseroles.

Breast is rather fatty and quite cheap. It is often sold whole. It can be boned, stuffed, and rolled, and then cooked slowly in the oven.

Middle end is normally sold as chops and has an excellent flavor—it is used in traditional Irish stew. The fat can be removed from the chops prior to cooking.

Scrag end is perhaps the cheapest cut and is not readily available nowadays due to its very fatty nature and low meat ratio.

Pork: the foreleg is a reasonably lean cut—it is often sold ready diced to use in casseroles or stews.

Belly is a fatty cut, which is sometimes sold salted. It can also be sold cut into ribs. Spare ribs contain the minimum of fat and can be used for roasting as well as in casseroles.

Other ingredients

Dried beans: these need to be soaked for at least 8 hours, preferably overnight, before cooking. After soaking, some beans, such as red kidney beans, need to be boiled rapidly for 10 minutes to remove toxins before cooking in the usual way.

Root vegetables: carrots, turnips, rutabagas, and parsnips are ideal vegetables to use in casseroles. During the long, slow cooking, the vegetables take on the flavor of the other strongly flavored ingredients, such as meat and seasonings. Other vegetables, such as celery, celeriac, tomatoes, and bell peppers, are also good.

Herbs: use dried herbs at the beginning of the cooking time, then add fresh herbs at the end. The best herbs to use are thyme, sage, parsley, bay, rosemary, oregano, and marjoram. A bouquet garni also makes a good addition to any casserole or stew.

KEY

 Simplicity level 1–3 (1 easiest, 3 slightly harder)

 Preparation time

 Cooking time

Green Vegetable Soup

This soup takes advantage of summer vegetables bursting with flavor.
If you find fresh small cannellini or other fresh beans, be sure to use them.

NUTRITIONAL INFORMATION

Calories	260	Sugars	. . . . .7g
Protein	. . . . .12g	Fat	. . . . .15g
Carbohydrate	. . .21g	Saturates	. . . . . . .4g

 15 mins   45 mins

SERVES 6

I N G R E D I E N T S

1 tbsp olive oil

1 onion, finely chopped

1 large leek, split and thinly sliced

1 celery stalk, thinly sliced

1 carrot, cut into fourths and thinly sliced

1 garlic clove, finely chopped

6 cups water

1 potato, diced

1 parsnip, finely diced

1 small kohlrabi or turnip, diced

5½ oz/150 g green beans, cut into
small pieces

5½ oz/150 g fresh or frozen peas

2 small zucchini, cut into fourths lengthwise
and sliced

14 oz/400 g canned small cannellini beans,
drained and rinsed

3½ oz/100 g spinach leaves, cut into
thin ribbons

salt and pepper

P E S T O

1 large garlic clove, very finely chopped

½ cup fresh basil leaves

1 cup freshly grated Parmesan cheese

4 tbsp extra-virgin olive oil

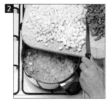  

1 Heat the oil in a large pan. Cook the onion and leek over low heat, stirring occasionally, for 5 minutes. Add the celery, carrot, and garlic, cover, and cook for another 5 minutes.

2 Add the water, potato, parsnip, kohlrabi or turnip, and green beans. Bring to a boil, lower the heat, cover, and simmer for 5 minutes.

3 Add the peas, zucchini, and small cannellini beans and season to taste.

Cover and simmer for about 25 minutes, until all the vegetables are tender.

4 Meanwhile, make the pesto. Put all the ingredients in a food processor and process until smooth, scraping down the sides as necessary. Alternatively, pound together using a pestle and mortar.

5 Add the spinach to the soup and simmer for 5 minutes. Stir a spoonful of the pesto into the soup. Ladle into bowls and serve the remaining pesto separately.

Crab & Cabbage Soup

From the Vera Cruz region of Mexico, this delicious soup uses fresh crab meat to add a rich flavor to a mildly spicy vegetable and fish broth.

NUTRITIONAL INFORMATION

Calories 131	Sugars 10g	
Protein 13g	Fat 4g	
Carbohydrate . . .12g	Saturates 0g	

🦐 25 mins   🕐 35 mins

SERVES 4

INGREDIENTS

¼ cabbage

1 lb/450 g ripe tomatoes

4 cups fish bouillon, or 4 cups boiling water mixed with 1–2 fish bouillon cubes

1 onion, thinly sliced

1 small carrot, diced

4 garlic cloves, finely chopped

6 tbsp chopped fresh cilantro

1 tsp mild chili powder

1 whole cooked crab or 6–8 oz/175–225 g crab meat

1 tbsp torn fresh oregano leaves

salt and pepper

TO SERVE

1–2 limes, cut into wedges

salsa of your choice

1 Cut out and discard any thick stalks from the cabbage, then shred the leaves finely using a large knife.

2 To skin the tomatoes, place in a heatproof bowl, pour boiling water over to cover, and let stand for about 30 seconds. Drain and plunge into cold water. The skins will then slide off easily. Coarsely chop the skinned tomatoes.

3 Place the tomatoes and bouillon in a pan with the onion, carrot, cabbage, garlic, fresh cilantro, and chili powder. Bring to a boil, then lower the heat and simmer for about 20 minutes, until the vegetables are just tender.

4 If using whole crab, remove and reserve the crab meat. Twist off the legs and claws and crack with a heavy knife. Remove the flesh from the legs with a skewer; leave the cracked claws intact, if desired. Remove the body section from the main crab shell and remove the meat, discarding the stomach sac and feathery gills that lie along each side of the body.

5 Add the crab meat and oregano leaves to the pan and simmer for 10–15 minutes to combine the flavors. Season to taste with salt and pepper.

6 Ladle into deep soup bowls and serve immediately with 1–2 wedges of lime per serving. Hand around a bowl of your chosen salsa separately.

Rice Soup with Eggs

This version of a classic Thai soup, sometimes eaten for breakfast, is a good way of using up any leftover cooked rice.

NUTRITIONAL INFORMATION

Calories	197	Sugars	.........1g
Protein	........11g	Fat	..........10g
Carbohydrate	...17g	Saturates	.......2g

🍲 5 mins   🕐 10 mins

SERVES 4

INGREDIENTS

1 tsp sunflower oil

1 garlic clove, crushed

½ cup ground pork

3 scallions, sliced

1 tbsp grated fresh gingerroot

1 fresh red bird-eye chile, seeded and chopped

4 cups chicken bouillon

generous 1 cup cooked long-grain rice

1 tbsp Thai fish sauce

4 small eggs

salt and pepper

2 tbsp shredded fresh cilantro, to garnish

1 Heat the oil in a large pan or wok. Add the garlic and pork and cook gently, stirring constantly, for about 1 minute, until the meat is broken up but not browned.

2 Stir in the scallions, ginger, chile, and bouillon and bring to a boil, stirring constantly. Add the rice, lower the heat, and simmer for 2 minutes.

3 Add the fish sauce and season to taste with salt and pepper. Carefully break the eggs into the soup and then simmer over very low heat for about 3–4 minutes, until set.

4 Ladle the soup into large, warmed bowls, allowing 1 egg per portion. Garnish with shredded fresh cilantro and serve immediately.

COOK'S TIP

If you prefer, beat the eggs together and cook like an omelet until set, then cut into ribbon-like strips and add to the soup just before serving.

Lentil & Rice Casserole

This is a really hearty dish, perfect for cold days when a filling hot dish is just what you need to keep the winter out.

 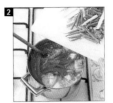 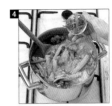

NUTRITIONAL INFORMATION

Calories	312	Sugars	.........9g
Protein	........20g	Fat	...........2g
Carbohydrate	...51g	Saturates	.....0.4g

15 mins   40 mins

SERVES 4

INGREDIENTS

1 cup split red lentils

generous ¼ cup long-grain rice

5 cups vegetable bouillon

1 leek, cut into chunks

3 garlic cloves, crushed

14 oz/400 g canned chopped tomatoes

1 tsp ground cumin

1 tsp chili powder

1 tsp garam masala

1 red bell pepper, seeded and sliced

3½ oz/100 g small broccoli florets

8 baby corn cobs, halved lengthwise

2 oz/55 g green beans, halved

1 tbsp shredded fresh basil

salt and pepper

sprigs of fresh basil, to garnish

1 Place the lentils, rice, and vegetable bouillon in a large flameproof casserole and cook over low heat, stirring occasionally, for 20 minutes.

2 Add the leek, garlic, tomatoes and their juice, ground cumin, chili powder, garam masala, sliced bell pepper, broccoli, corn cobs, and green beans to the casserole.

3 Bring the mixture to a boil, lower the heat, cover, and simmer for another 10–15 minutes, or until all the vegetables are tender.

4 Add the shredded basil and season with salt and pepper to taste.

5 Garnish with fresh basil sprigs and serve immediately.

VARIATION

You can vary the rice in this recipe—use brown or wild rice, if you prefer.

Winter Vegetable Pot Pie

Seasonal fresh vegetables are casseroled with lentils, then topped with a ring of fresh cheese biscuits to make this tasty pot pie.

NUTRITIONAL INFORMATION

Calories 734   Sugars 22g
Protein . . . . .27g   Fat 30g
Carbohydrate . . .96g   Saturates 16g

🥘 20 mins   🕐 40 mins

SERVES 4

I N G R E D I E N T S

1 tbsp olive oil

1 garlic clove, crushed

8 small onions, halved

2 celery stalks, sliced

8 oz/225 g rutabaga, chopped

2 carrots, sliced

½ small cauliflower, broken into florets

3¼ cups sliced mushrooms

14 oz/400 g canned chopped tomatoes

¼ cup red lentils

2 tbsp cornstarch

3–4 tbsp water

1¼ cups vegetable bouillon

2 tsp Tabasco sauce

2 tsp chopped fresh oregano

sprigs of fresh oregano, to garnish

P O T   P I E   T O P P I N G

2 cups self-rising flour

4 tbsp butter

1 cup grated sharp colby cheese

2 tsp chopped fresh oregano

1 egg, lightly beaten

⅔ cup milk

salt

1 Heat the oil in a large skillet and cook the garlic and onions for 5 minutes. Add the celery, rutabaga, carrots, and cauliflower and cook for 2–3 minutes. Add the mushrooms, tomatoes, and lentils. Mix the cornstarch and water together and stir into the pan with the bouillon, Tabasco, and oregano. Transfer to a casserole and cover.

2 Bake in a preheated oven, 350°F/ 180°C, for 20 minutes.

3 To make the topping, sift the flour with a pinch of salt into a bowl. Rub in the butter, then stir in most of the cheese and the chopped oregano. Beat the egg with the milk and add enough to the dry ingredients to make a soft dough. Knead lightly, roll out to ½ inch/1 cm thick and cut into 2-inch/5-cm circles.

4 Remove the casserole from the oven and increase the temperature to 400°F/200°C. Arrange the biscuits around the edge of the casserole, brush with the remaining egg and milk, and sprinkle with the reserved cheese. Cook for another 10–12 minutes. Garnish and serve.

Coconut Vegetable Curry

A mildly spiced but richly flavored Indian-style dish full of different textures and flavors. Serve with nan bread to soak up the tasty sauce.

NUTRITIONAL INFORMATION

Calories ....159 Sugars 8g
Protein ....8g Fat 6g
Carbohydrate ...19g Saturates 1g

1¾ hrs   35 mins

SERVES 4

INGREDIENTS

1 large eggplant, cut into 1-inch/
   2.5-cm cubes

2 tbsp vegetable oil

2 garlic cloves, crushed

1 fresh green chile, seeded and
   finely chopped

1 tsp grated fresh gingerroot

1 onion, finely chopped

2 tsp garam masala

8 cardamom pods

1 tsp ground turmeric

1 tbsp tomato paste

3 cups vegetable bouillon

1 tbsp lemon juice

8 oz/225 g potatoes, diced

9 oz/250 g small cauliflower florets

8 oz/225 g okra, trimmed

2 cups frozen peas

⅔ cup coconut milk

salt and pepper

flaked coconut, to garnish

nan bread, to serve

1 Layer the eggplant in a bowl, sprinkling with salt as you go. Set aside for 30 minutes. Rinse well under running water. Drain and dry. Set aside.

2 Heat the oil in a large pan and gently cook the garlic, chile, ginger, onion, and spices for 4–5 minutes.

3 Stir in the tomato paste, bouillon, lemon juice, potatoes, and cauliflower and mix well. Bring to a boil, cover, and simmer for 15 minutes.

4 Stir in the eggplant, okra, peas, and coconut milk and season with salt and pepper to taste. Continue to simmer, uncovered, for another 10 minutes, until tender. Discard the cardamom pods. Pile the curry onto a warmed serving platter, garnish with flaked coconut, and serve with nan bread.

Shellfish in Red Curry Sauce

For something very quick and simple that sets your taste buds alight, try this inspired dish of shrimp in a marvelously spicy sauce.

NUTRITIONAL INFORMATION

Calories	175	Sugars	........3g
Protein	........29g	Fat	..........5g
Carbohydrate	....3g	Saturates	......1g

10 mins

10 mins

SERVES 4

INGREDIENTS

1 tbsp vegetable oil

6 scallions, sliced

1 lemongrass stalk

½-inch/1-cm piece of fresh gingerroot

generous 1 cup coconut milk

2 tbsp Thai red curry paste

1 tbsp Thai fish sauce

1 lb 2 oz/500 g raw jumbo shrimp

1 tbsp chopped fresh cilantro

fresh chiles, to garnish

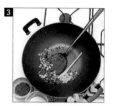

VARIATION

Try this recipe using Thai green curry sauce instead of red. Both varieties are obtainable from many supermarkets—look for them in the Asian foods section.

1 Heat the vegetable oil in a wok or large skillet. Add the scallions and cook over low heat for about 2 minutes, until softened.

2 Bruise the stalk of lemongrass using a meat mallet or rolling pin. Peel and finely grate the fresh gingerroot.

3 Add the lemongrass and ginger to the wok or skillet with the coconut milk, Thai red curry paste, and Thai fish sauce. Heat gently, until the coconut milk is almost boiling.

4 Peel the shrimp, leaving the tails intact. Remove the black vein along the back of each shrimp.

5 Add the shrimp to the wok or skillet with the chopped cilantro and cook gently for 5 minutes.

6 Transfer the shrimp with the sauce to a warm serving bowl, garnish with fresh chiles, and serve immediately.

Spanish Fish Stew

This is an impressive-looking Catalan dish using two classic Spanish cooking methods—the *sofrito* and the *picada*.

NUTRITIONAL INFORMATION

Calories	346	Sugars 4g
Protein	........37g	Fat 13g
Carbohydrate	....11g	Saturates 2g

30 mins · 1 hr

SERVES 6

I N G R E D I E N T S

5 tbsp olive oil

2 large onions, finely chopped

2 tomatoes, skinned, seeded, and diced

2 slices white bread, crusts removed

4 almonds, toasted

3 garlic cloves, coarsely chopped

12 oz/350 g cooked lobster

7 oz/200 g cleaned squid

7 oz/200 g monkfish fillet

7 oz/200 g cod fillet, skinned

1 tbsp all-purpose flour

6 large raw shrimp

6 langoustines

18 live mussels, scrubbed, and beards removed

8 large live clams, scrubbed

1 tbsp chopped fresh parsley

½ cup brandy

salt and pepper

 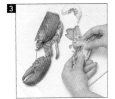 

1 Heat 3 tablespoons of the oil and cook the onions gently for about 10–15 minutes, until lightly golden. Add the tomatoes and cook until softened.

2 Heat 1 tablespoon of the remaining oil and cook the slices of bread until crisp. Break into pieces and put into a mortar with the almonds and 2 garlic cloves. Pound to a fine paste. Alternatively, process in a food processor.

3 Split the lobster lengthwise. Remove and discard the intestinal vein, the stomach sac, and the spongy gills. Crack the claws and remove the meat. Take out the flesh from the tail and chop into large chunks. Slice the squid into rings.

4 Season the monkfish, cod, and lobster and dust with flour. Heat a little of the remaining oil and separately brown the monkfish, cod, lobster, squid, shrimp, and langoustines. Arrange them in a flameproof casserole as they brown.

5 Add the mussels and clams, the remaining garlic, and the parsley. Set the pan over low heat. Pour over the brandy and ignite. When the flames have died down, add the tomato mixture and just enough water to cover. Bring to a boil and simmer for 3–4 minutes, until the mussels and clams have opened. Stir in the bread mixture and season. Simmer for another 5 minutes and serve.

Moroccan Fish Tagine

A tagine is a Moroccan cooking vessel consisting of an earthenware dish with a domed lid that has a steam hole in the top.

NUTRITIONAL INFORMATION

Calories	188	Sugars 5g
Protein	........17g	Fat 11g
Carbohydrate	....7g	Saturates 1g

10 mins   1¼ hrs

SERVES 4

I N G R E D I E N T S

2 tbsp olive oil

1 large onion, finely chopped

pinch of saffron threads

½ tsp ground cinnamon

1 tsp ground coriander

½ tsp ground cumin

½ tsp ground turmeric

7 oz/200 g canned chopped tomatoes

1¼ cups fish bouillon

4 small red snapper, cleaned, boned, and heads and tails removed

½ cup pitted green olives

1 tbsp chopped preserved lemon (see Cook's Tip, below)

3 tbsp chopped fresh cilantro

salt and pepper

couscous, to serve

COOK'S TIP

For preserved lemons, take enough lemons to fill a preserving jar. Cut them into fourths lengthwise, without cutting all the way through. Pack them with ¼ cup sea salt per lemon. Add the juice of 1 more lemon and top up with water to cover. Leave for 1 month.

1 Heat the olive oil in a large pan or flameproof casserole. Add the onion and cook gently, stirring occasionally, for 10 minutes without coloring, until softened. Add the saffron, cinnamon, ground coriander, cumin, and turmeric and cook for another 30 seconds, stirring.

2 Add the chopped tomatoes and fish bouillon and stir well. Bring to a boil, cover, and simmer for 15 minutes. Uncover and simmer for another 20–35 minutes, until thickened.

3 Cut each red snapper in half, then add the pieces to the pan, pushing them into the sauce. Simmer gently for another 5–6 minutes, until the fish is just cooked.

4 Carefully stir in the olives, preserved lemon, and the chopped cilantro. Season to taste and serve with couscous.

Stewed Sardines

This is an unusual stew of sardines cooked with baby onions, tomatoes, olives, raisins, Marsala, and pine nuts.

NUTRITIONAL INFORMATION

Calories . . . . .412 Sugars 14g
Protein . . . . .26g Fat 27g
Carbohydrate . . .15g Saturates 5g

 1¼ hrs   50 mins

SERVES 4

I N G R E D I E N T S

scant ½ cup raisins

3 tbsp Marsala

4 tbsp olive oil

8 oz/225 g baby onions, halved if large

2 garlic cloves, chopped

1 tbsp chopped fresh sage

4 large tomatoes, skinned and chopped

⅔ cup fish bouillon or vegetable bouillon

2 tbsp balsamic vinegar

1 lb/450 g fresh sardines, cleaned

¼ cup pitted black olives

¼ cup pine nuts, toasted

2 tbsp chopped fresh parsley

1 Put the raisins in a small bowl and pour over the Marsala. Set aside to soak for about 1 hour, until the raisins are plump. Strain, reserving both the Marsala and the raisins.

2 Heat the olive oil in a large pan and cook the onions over low heat for 15 minutes, until golden and tender. Add the garlic and chopped sage and cook for another minute.

3 Add the tomatoes, cook for another 2–3 minutes, then add the bouillon, vinegar, and reserved Marsala. Bring to a boil, cover, and simmer for 25 minutes.

4 Add the sardines and simmer gently for 2–3 minutes before adding the raisins, olives, and pine nuts. Simmer for 2–3 minutes, until the sardines are cooked. Add the chopped parsley and serve immediately.

VARIATIONS
You can substitute smoked cod for the sardines in this recipe, if you prefer.

Fish with Black Bean Sauce

Steaming is one of the preferred methods of cooking whole fish in China because it maintains both the flavor and the texture.

NUTRITIONAL INFORMATION

Calories	292	Sugars	.........3g
Protein	........44g	Fat	..........7g
Carbohydrate	....6g	Saturates	.....0.4g

🍲 10 mins   ⏱ 10 mins

SERVES 4

I N G R E D I E N T S

2 lb/900 g whole snapper, cleaned and scaled

3 garlic cloves, crushed

2 tbsp black bean sauce

1 tsp cornstarch

2 tsp sesame oil

2 tbsp light soy sauce

2 tsp superfine sugar

2 tbsp dry sherry

1 small leek, shredded

1 small red bell pepper, seeded and cut into thin strips

shredded leek and lemon wedges, to garnish

boiled rice or noodles, to serve

1 Rinse the fish inside and out with cold running water and pat dry with paper towels.

2 Make 2–3 diagonal slashes in the flesh on each side of the fish, using a sharp knife. Rub the garlic into the fish.

3 Combine the black bean sauce, cornstarch, sesame oil, light soy sauce, sugar, and dry sherry.

4 Place the fish in a shallow heatproof dish and pour the sauce mixture over the top. Sprinkle the shredded leek and bell pepper strips on top of the sauce.

5 Place the dish in the top of a steamer, cover, and steam for 10 minutes, or until the fish is cooked through.

6 Transfer the fish to a serving dish, garnish with shredded leek and lemon wedges, and serve immediately with boiled rice or noodles.

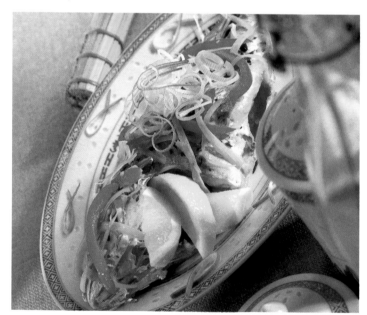

COOK'S TIP

Insert the point of a sharp knife into the fish to test if it is cooked. The fish is cooked through if the knife goes into the flesh easily.

Thai Green Fish Curry

This pale green curry paste can be used as the basis for all sorts of Thai dishes. It is also delicious with chicken and beef.

NUTRITIONAL INFORMATION

Calories 217	Sugars 3g	
Protein 12g	Fat 17g	
Carbohydrate 5g	Saturates 10g	

15 mins   15 mins

SERVES 4

INGREDIENTS

2 tbsp vegetable oil

1 garlic clove, chopped

1 small eggplant, diced

½ cup coconut cream

2 tbsp Thai fish sauce

1 tsp sugar

8 oz/225 g firm white fish, cut into pieces, such as cod, haddock, or halibut

½ cup fish bouillon

2 kaffir lime leaves, finely shredded

about 15 leaves Thai basil, if available, or ordinary basil

plain boiled rice or noodles, to serve

GREEN CURRY PASTE

5 fresh green chiles, seeded and chopped

2 tsp chopped lemongrass

1 large shallot, chopped

2 garlic cloves, chopped

1 tsp grated fresh gingerroot or galangal

2 fresh cilantro roots, chopped

½ tsp ground coriander

¼ tsp ground cumin

1 kaffir lime leaf, finely chopped

1 tsp shrimp paste (optional)

½ tsp salt

1 To make the curry paste, put all the ingredients into a blender or spice grinder and blend to a smooth paste, adding a little water if necessary. Alternatively, pound together all the ingredients, using a mortar and pestle, until smooth. Set aside.

2 Heat the oil in a skillet or wok, until almost smoking. Add the garlic and cook until golden. Add the curry paste and stir-fry for a few seconds before adding the eggplant. Stir-fry for about 4–5 minutes, until softened.

3 Add the coconut cream. Bring to a boil and stir until the cream thickens and curdles slightly. Add the fish sauce and sugar and stir into the mixture.

4 Add the fish pieces and bouillon. Simmer, stirring occasionally, for 3–4 minutes, until the fish is just tender. Add the lime leaves and basil and then cook for another minute.

5 Transfer the curry to a warmed serving dish and serve with plain boiled rice or noodles.

Cotriade

This is a rich French stew of fish and vegetables, flavored with saffron and herbs. The fish and vegetables, and the soup, are served separately.

NUTRITIONAL INFORMATION

Calories 81   Sugars 0.9g
Protein . . . . . . .7.4g   Fat 3.9g
Carbohydrate . . .3.8g   Saturates 1.1g

🄶 🄶 🄶

15 mins   🕐 40 mins

SERVES 4

I N G R E D I E N T S

pinch of saffron

2½ cups hot fish bouillon

1 tbsp olive oil

2 tbsp butter

1 onion, sliced

2 garlic cloves, chopped

1 leek, sliced

1 small fennel bulb, thinly sliced

1 lb/450 g potatoes, cut into chunks

⅔ cup dry white wine

1 tbsp fresh thyme leaves

2 bay leaves

4 ripe tomatoes, skinned and chopped

2 lb/900 g mixed fish fillets, such as
   haddock, hake, mackerel, or red mullet,
   coarsely chopped

2 tbsp chopped fresh parsley

salt and pepper

crusty bread, to serve

1 Using a mortar and pestle, crush the saffron and add it to the fish bouillon. Stir the mixture and set aside to steep for at least 10 minutes.

2 Heat the olive oil and butter together in a large, heavy-bottomed pan. Add the onion and cook over low heat, stirring occasionally, for 4–5 minutes, until softened but not browned. Add the garlic, leek, fennel, and potatoes. Cover and cook for another 10–15 minutes, until the vegetables are softened.

3 Add the white wine and simmer rapidly for 3–4 minutes, until it has reduced by about half. Add the thyme, bay leaves, and tomatoes and stir well. Add the saffron-steeped fish bouillon. Bring to a boil, cover, and simmer over low heat for about 15 minutes, until all the vegetables are tender.

4 Add the fish, return to a boil, and simmer for another 3–4 minutes, until all the fish is tender. Add the parsley and season to taste. Using a slotted spoon, remove the fish and vegetables to a warmed serving dish. Serve the soup with plenty of crusty bread.

VARIATION

Once the fish and vegetables have been cooked, you could process the soup in a food processor or blender and pass it through a strainer to give a smooth fish soup.

Chicken & Potato Casserole

Small new potatoes are ideal for this recipe because they can be cooked whole. If larger potatoes are used, cut them in half or into chunks.

NUTRITIONAL INFORMATION

Calories ....856 Sugars 7g
Protein ....35g Fat 58g
Carbohydrate ...40g Saturates 26g

 5 mins   1½ hrs

SERVES 4

I N G R E D I E N T S

2 tbsp vegetable oil

5 tbsp butter

4 chicken portions, about 8 oz/225 g each

2 leeks, sliced

1 garlic clove, crushed

4 tbsp all-purpose flour

3¾ cups chicken bouillon

1¼ cups dry white wine

4 oz/115 g baby carrots, halved lengthwise

4 oz/115 g baby corn cobs, halved lengthwise

1 lb/450 g small new potatoes

1 bouquet garni

⅔ cup heavy cream

salt and pepper

boiled rice or fresh vegetables, to serve

1 Heat the oil and butter in a large skillet. Cook the chicken for 10 minutes, turning, until browned all over. Transfer the chicken to a casserole.

2 Add the leeks and garlic to the skillet and cook for 2–3 minutes, stirring constantly. Stir in the flour and cook for another minute, stirring constantly. Remove the skillet from the heat and stir in the bouillon and wine. Season well.

3 Return the skillet to the heat and bring the mixture to a boil. Stir in the carrots, baby corn cobs, new potatoes, and bouquet garni.

4 Transfer the mixture to the casserole. Cover and cook in a preheated oven, 350°F/180°C, for about 1 hour.

5 Remove the casserole from the oven and stir in the cream. Return the casserole to the oven, uncovered, and cook for another 15 minutes. Remove the bouquet garni and discard. Taste and adjust the seasoning, if necessary. Serve the casserole with boiled rice or fresh vegetables, such as broccoli.

COOK'S TIP

Use turkey fillets instead of the chicken, if preferred, and vary the vegetables according to those you have at hand.

Chicken & Chili Bean Pot

This aromatic chicken dish has a spicy Mexican kick. Chicken thighs have a marvelous flavor when cooked in this way.

NUTRITIONAL INFORMATION

Calories 333	Sugars 10g	
Protein 25g	Fat 13g	
Carbohydrate ...32g	Saturates 2g	

 10 mins   40 mins

SERVES 4

I N G R E D I E N T S

2 tbsp all-purpose flour

1 tsp chili powder

8 chicken thighs or 4 chicken legs

3 tbsp vegetable oil

2 garlic cloves, crushed

1 large onion, chopped

1 green or red bell pepper, seeded and chopped

1¼ cups chicken bouillon

12 oz/350 g tomatoes, chopped

14 oz/400 g canned red kidney beans, rinsed and drained

2 tbsp tomato paste

salt and pepper

1 Combine the flour and chili powder in a shallow dish and add salt and pepper to taste. Rinse the chicken, but do not dry. Dip the chicken into the seasoned flour, turning to coat it on all sides.

2 Heat the oil in a large, deep skillet or flameproof casserole and add the chicken. Cook over high heat, turning the pieces frequently, for 3–4 minutes, until browned all over.

3 Lift the chicken out of the skillet or casserole with a slotted spoon and drain on paper towels.

4 Add the garlic, onion, and bell pepper to the skillet or casserole and cook over medium heat, stirring occasionally, for 2–3 minutes, until softened.

5 Add the bouillon, tomatoes, kidney beans, and tomato paste, stirring well. Bring to a boil, then return the chicken to the pan. Lower the heat, cover, and simmer for about 30 minutes, until the chicken is tender. Taste and adjust the seasoning, if necessary, and serve.

COOK'S TIP

For extra intensity of flavor, use sun-dried tomato paste instead of ordinary tomato paste.

Rustic Chicken & Orange Pot

Low in fat and high in fiber, this colorful casserole makes a healthy, hearty, and utterly delicious one-pot meal.

NUTRITIONAL INFORMATION

Calories 345	Sugars 6g	
Protein 29g	Fat 10g	
Carbohydrate ...39g	Saturates 2g	

🍲 5 mins   🕐 1 hr

SERVES 4

I N G R E D I E N T S

8 skinless chicken drumsticks

1 tbsp whole-wheat flour

1 tbsp olive oil

2 medium red onions

1 garlic clove, crushed

1 tsp fennel seeds

1 bay leaf

finely grated rind and juice of
   1 small orange

14 oz/400 g canned chopped tomatoes

14 oz/400 g canned cannellini or small navy
   beans, drained

salt and black pepper

TOPPING

3 thick slices whole-wheat bread,
   crusts removed

2 tsp olive oil

1 Toss the chicken in the flour to coat evenly. Heat the oil in a nonstick pan. Add the chicken and cook over fairly high heat, turning frequently, until golden brown. Transfer to a large casserole.

2 Cut the red onions into thin wedges. Add to the pan and cook over medium heat for a few minutes, until lightly browned. Stir in the garlic, then add the onions and garlic to the casserole.

3 Add the fennel seeds, bay leaf, orange rind and juice, tomatoes, and cannellini or small navy beans and season to taste with salt and pepper.

4 Cover tightly and cook in a preheated oven, 375°F/ 190°C, for 30–35 minutes, until the chicken juices are clear and not pink when pierced through the thickest part with a skewer.

5 To make the topping, cut the bread into small cubes and toss in the oil. Remove the lid from the casserole and sprinkle the bread cubes on top of the chicken. Bake for another 15–20 minutes, until the bread is golden and crisp. Serve immediately straight from the casserole.

Chicken Basquaise

Sweet bell peppers are typical of dishes from the Basque region in France. In this recipe, Bayonne ham, from the Pyrenees, adds a delicious flavor.

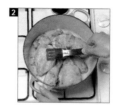

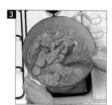

NUTRITIONAL INFORMATION

Calories 559	Sugars 8g	
Protein 50g	Fat 21g	
Carbohydrate ...44g	Saturates 6g	

15 mins   1½ hrs

SERVES 4–5

INGREDIENTS

3 lb/1.3 kg chicken, cut into 8 pieces

2 tbsp all-purpose flour, for dusting

2–3 tbsp olive oil

1 Bermuda onion, thickly sliced

2 red or yellow bell peppers, seeded and cut lengthwise into thick strips

2 garlic cloves

5½ oz/150 g spicy chorizo sausage, peeled and cut into ½-inch/1-cm pieces

1 tbsp tomato paste

1 cup long-grain white rice

2 cups chicken bouillon

1 tsp crushed dried chilies

½ tsp dried thyme

¾ cup diced Bayonne or other air-dried ham

12 dry-cured black olives

2 tbsp chopped fresh flatleaf parsley

salt and pepper

1 Pat the chicken pieces dry with paper towels. Put 2 tablespoons flour in a plastic bag, season with salt and pepper, and add the chicken pieces. Seal the bag and shake to coat the chicken.

2 Heat 2 tablespoons of olive oil in a large, flameproof casserole over medium-high heat. Add the chicken and cook, turning frequently, for about 15 minutes, until well browned all over. Transfer to a plate.

3 Heat the remaining oil in the casserole and add the onion and red or yellow bell peppers. Lower the heat to medium and stir-fry, until beginning to color and soften. Add the garlic, chorizo, and tomato paste and cook, stirring constantly, for about 3 minutes. Add the rice and cook, stirring to coat, for about 2 minutes, until the rice is translucent.

4 Add the bouillon, crushed chilies, and thyme, season to taste with salt and pepper, and stir well. Bring to a boil. Return the chicken to the casserole, pressing it gently into the rice. Cover and cook over very low heat for about 45 minutes, until the chicken is cooked through and the rice is tender.

5 Gently stir the ham, black olives, and half the parsley into the rice mixture. Re-cover and heat through for another 5 minutes. Sprinkle with the remaining parsley and serve immediately.

Chicken & Noodle One Pot

Flavorsome chicken and vegetables are cooked with Chinese egg noodles in a coconut sauce. Serve in deep soup bowls.

NUTRITIONAL INFORMATION

Calories	256	Sugars 7g
Protein	........30g	Fat 8g
Carbohydrate	...18g	Saturates 2g

5 mins   20 mins

SERVES 4

I N G R E D I E N T S

1 tbsp sunflower oil

1 onion, sliced

1 garlic clove, crushed

1-inch/2.5-cm piece of fresh gingerroot, grated

bunch of scallions, sliced diagonally

1 lb 2 oz/500 g skinless chicken breast fillet, cut into bite-size pieces

2 tbsp mild curry paste

2 cups coconut milk

1¼ cups chicken bouillon

9 oz/250 g Chinese egg noodles

2 tsp lime juice

salt and pepper

sprigs of fresh basil, to garnish

1 Heat the sunflower oil in a wok or large, heavy skillet.

2 Add the onion, garlic, ginger, and scallions and stir-fry over medium heat for 2 minutes, until softened.

3 Add the chicken and curry paste and stir-fry for 4 minutes, or until the vegetables and chicken are golden brown. Stir in the coconut milk, bouillon, and salt and pepper to taste and mix well.

4 Bring to a boil, break the noodles into large pieces, if necessary, and add to the wok or pan. Cover and simmer, stirring occasionally, for about 6–8 minutes, until the noodles are just tender.

5 Add the lime juice and adjust the seasoning if necessary.

6 Serve the chicken and noodle one pot immediately in deep soup bowls, garnished with basil sprigs.

COOK'S TIP

If you enjoy hot flavors, substitute the mild curry paste in this recipe with hot curry paste (found in most supermarkets) but reduce the quantity to 1 tablespoon.

Beef & Orange Curry

A spicy blend of tender chunks of succulent beef with the tang of orange and the warmth of Indian spices.

NUTRITIONAL INFORMATION

Calories	345	Sugars	........24g
Protein	........28g	Fat	..........13g
Carbohydrate	...31g	Saturates	......3g

15 mins 1¼ hrs

SERVES 4

INGREDIENTS

1 tbsp vegetable oil

8 oz/225 g shallots, halved

2 garlic cloves, crushed

1 lb/450 g lean round steak or sirloin beef, trimmed and cut into ¾-inch/2-cm cubes

3 tbsp curry paste

2 cups beef bouillon

4 medium oranges

2 tsp cornstarch

salt and pepper

2 tbsp chopped fresh cilantro, to garnish

boiled basmati rice, to serve

RAITA

½ cucumber, finely diced

3 tbsp chopped fresh mint

⅔ cup lowfat plain yogurt

1 Heat the oil in a large pan. Add the shallots, garlic, and beef cubes and cook over low heat, stirring occasionally, for 5 minutes, until the beef is evenly browned all over.

2 Blend together the curry paste and bouillon. Add the mixture to the beef and stir to mix thoroughly. Bring to a boil, cover, and simmer for about 1 hour.

3 Grate the rind of 1 orange. Squeeze the juice from the orange and from 1 other. Peel the other 2 oranges, removing the pith. Slice between each segment and remove the flesh.

4 Blend the cornstarch with the orange juice. At the end of the cooking time, stir the orange rind into the beef with the orange and cornstarch mixture. Bring to a boil and simmer, stirring constantly, for 3–4 minutes, until the sauce thickens. Season to taste with salt and pepper and stir in the orange segments.

5 To make the raita, mix the cucumber with the mint and stir in the yogurt. Season with salt and pepper to taste.

6 Garnish the curry with the chopped cilantro and serve with boiled rice and the cucumber raita.

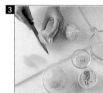

Beef Korma with Almonds

This korma, a traditional northern Indian recipe, has a thick, richly flavored, creamy textured sauce and is quite simple to cook.

NUTRITIONAL INFORMATION

Calories 735   Sugars 6g
Protein . . . . .41g   Fat 60g
Carbohydrate . . . .9g   Saturates 9g

🍲 20 mins   🕐 1½ hrs

SERVES 4

INGREDIENTS

1¼ cups vegetable oil

3 medium onions, finely chopped

2 lb 4 oz/1 kg lean beef, cubed

1½ tsp garam masala

1½ tsp ground coriander

1½ tsp finely chopped fresh gingerroot

1½ tsp crushed garlic

1 tsp salt

⅔ cup plain yogurt

2 cloves

3 green cardamoms

4 black peppercorns

2½ cups water

chapatis, to serve

TO GARNISH

6 almonds, soaked, peeled, and chopped

2 fresh green chiles, chopped

a few fresh cilantro leaves

1 Heat the oil in a skillet. Add the onions and stir-fry, until golden brown. Remove half of the onions from the pan and reserve.

2 Add the meat to the remaining onions in the pan and stir-fry for about 5 minutes. Remove the pan from the heat.

3 Combine the garam masala, ground coriander, ginger, garlic, salt, and yogurt in a bowl. Gradually add the meat to the spice mixture and mix to coat well. Return the meat mixture to the pan. Cook, stirring constantly, for 5–7 minutes, or until the mixture is golden.

4 Add the cloves, cardamoms, and peppercorns. Pour in the water, lower the heat, cover the pan, and simmer for 45–60 minutes. If necessary, add another 1¼ cups water and then cook for another 10–15 minutes, stirring occasionally.

5 Just before serving, garnish with the reserved onions, chopped almonds, green chiles, and the fresh cilantro leaves. Serve with chapatis.

Michoacan Beef

This rich, smoky-flavored Mexican stew is delicious;
leftovers make a great filling for tacos, too.

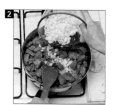

NUTRITIONAL INFORMATION

Calories . . . . .315 Sugars 6g
Protein . . . . .41g Fat 10g
Carbohydrate . . .16g Saturates 3g

10 mins   2 hrs

SERVES 4–6

INGREDIENTS

about 3 tbsp all-purpose flour

2 lb 4 oz/1 kg stewing beef, cut into large,
bite-size pieces

2 tbsp vegetable oil

2 onions, chopped

5 garlic cloves, chopped

14 oz/400 g tomatoes, diced

1½ dried chipotle chilies, reconstituted,
seeded, and cut into thin strips, or a few
shakes of bottled chipotle salsa

6⅓ cups beef bouillon

12 oz/350 g green beans

salt and pepper

TO SERVE

simmered beans

cooked rice

COOK'S TIP

This is traditionally made
with *nopales* (edible cacti),
which give the dish a distinctive
flavor. Look for them in specialty
stores. For this recipe you need
12–14 oz/350–400 g canned
or fresh nopales.

1 Place the flour in a large bowl and
season with salt and pepper. Add the
beef and toss to coat well. Remove from
the bowl, shaking off the excess flour.

2 Heat the oil in a skillet and brown the
meat briefly over high heat. Lower the
heat to medium, add the onions and
garlic, and cook for 2 minutes.

3 Add the tomatoes, chilies, and bouillon.
Cover and simmer over low heat for
1½ hours, or until the meat is very tender,
adding the green beans 15 minutes before
the end of the cooking time. Skim off any
fat that rises to the surface.

4 Transfer to individual bowls and serve
with simmered beans and cooked rice.

Potato, Beef & Peanut Pot

The spicy peanut sauce in this recipe will complement almost any meat; the dish is just as delicious made with chicken or pork.

NUTRITIONAL INFORMATION

Calories 559	Sugars 5g	
Protein 35g	Fat 37g	
Carbohydrate ...24g	Saturates 13g	

🔺 5 mins 🕐 1 hr

SERVES 4

INGREDIENTS

1 tbsp vegetable oil

5 tbsp butter

1 lb/450 g lean steak, cut into thin strips

1 onion, halved and sliced

2 garlic cloves, crushed

1 lb 5 oz/600 g waxy potatoes, cubed

½ tsp paprika

4 tbsp crunchy peanut butter

2½ cups beef bouillon

4 tbsp unsalted peanuts

2 tsp light soy sauce

2 oz/55 g sugar snap peas

1 red bell pepper, seeded and sliced

sprigs of fresh parsley, to garnish (optional)

  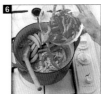

1 Heat the vegetable oil and butter in a flameproof casserole.

2 Add the steak strips and cook them gently for about 3–4 minutes, stirring and turning the meat, until it is seared on all sides.

3 Add the onion and garlic and cook for another 2 minutes, stirring constantly.

4 Add the potato cubes and cook for 3–4 minutes, or until they begin to brown slightly.

5 Stir in the paprika and peanut butter, then gradually stir in the beef bouillon. Bring the mixture to a boil, stirring frequently.

6 Finally, add the peanuts, soy sauce, sugar snap peas, and red bell pepper.

7 Cover and cook over low heat for 45 minutes, or until the beef is cooked right through.

8 Garnish the dish with parsley sprigs, if using. Serve immediately.

COOK'S TIP

Serve this dish with plain boiled rice or noodles, if you wish.

Spicy Pork with Prunes

Prunes add an earthy, wine flavor to this spicy stew.
Serve with tortillas or crusty bread to dip into the rich sauce.

NUTRITIONAL INFORMATION		
Calories 352	Sugars 1g	
Protein 39g	Fat 12g	
Carbohydrate . . .24g	Saturates 2g	

🕑 8¼ hrs   🕐 3–4 hrs

SERVES 4–6

I N G R E D I E N T S

3 lb 5 oz/1.5 kg pork joint, such as leg
  or shoulder

juice of 2–3 limes

10 garlic cloves, chopped

3–4 tbsp mild chili powder

4 tbsp vegetable oil

2 onions, chopped

2¼ cups chicken bouillon

25 small, tart tomatoes, coarsely chopped

25 prunes, pitted

1–2 tsp sugar

pinch of ground cinnamon

pinch of ground allspice

pinch of ground cumin

salt

warmed corn tortillas, to serve

1 Combine the pork with the lime juice, garlic, chili powder, 2 tablespoons of oil, and salt to taste. Set aside to marinate in the refrigerator overnight.

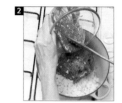

2 Remove the pork from the marinade. Wipe the pork dry with paper towels and reserve the marinade. Heat the remaining oil in a flameproof casserole and brown the pork evenly, until just golden. Add the onions, the reserved marinade, and the bouillon. Cover and cook in a preheated oven, 350°F/180°C, for about 2–3 hours, until tender.

3 Spoon off the fat from the surface of the cooking liquid and add the tomatoes. Continue to cook for about 20 minutes, until the tomatoes are tender. Mash the tomatoes into a coarse puree. Add the prunes and sugar, then adjust the seasoning. Add the cinnamon, allspice, and cumin to taste, as well as extra chili powder, if desired.

4 Increase the oven temperature to 400°F/200°C. Return the meat and sauce to the oven for another 20–30 minutes, or until the meat has browned on top and the juices have thickened.

5 Remove the meat and set aside for a few minutes. Carefully carve it into thin slices and spoon the sauce over the top. Serve warm with corn tortillas.